Rachel Horman is a Solicitor and Head of the Domestic Abuse, Stalking and Forced Marriage Department at Watson Ramsbottom Ltd. Rachel regularly advises clients on how to increase the chances of obtaining a successful prosecution for stalking and domestic abuse as well as advising in relation to civil options. She was personally involved in the campaign to change the law to create a criminal offence of coercive control or emotional abuse which came into force in December 2015 and continues to be involved in advising the police and government around other problems with the current law in relation to stalking and domestic abuse.

Rachel regularly represents clients with regard to coercive control within the family courts. She has practiced in the area of domestic abuse and stalking for over 20 years and heads a department dealing with these issues. She is the Chair of Paladin – the National Stalking Advocacy Service and is a regular media commentator on coercive control and stalking including BBC Breakfast, BBC News, Sky News and Radio 4 and is considered to be one of the leading subject matter experts in this area.

Rachel advises several prime time TV shows regarding scripts dealing with stalking and coercive control. She has won several awards for her work in these areas including the Jordans Family Law Partner of the Year and Legal Aid Lawyer of the Year as well as being highly commended by the Law Society in the Female Lawyer of the Year Category and shortlisted for the Emma Humphries Memorial Prize for her work in assisting victims of domestic abuse.

Rachel also writes a popular blog at rachelhorman.co.uk where she comments on new developments or gaps in the law around Domestic Abuse, Stalking and Honour Based Violence.

A Practical Guide to Coercive Control for Legal Practitioners and Victims

A Practical Guide to Coercive Control for Legal Practitioners and Victims

Rachel Horman LLB (Hons)
Solicitor and Director Watson Ramsbottom Ltd and Chair of Paladin

Law Brief Publishing

© Rachel Horman

All rights reserved. No part of this publication may be reproduced, stored in a retrieval system, or transmitted, in any form or by any means, electronic, mechanical, photocopying, recording or otherwise, without the prior permission of the publisher.

Excerpts from judgments and statutes are Crown copyright. Any Crown Copyright material is reproduced with the permission of the Controller of OPSI and the Queen's Printer for Scotland. Some quotations may be licensed under the terms of the Open Government Licence (http://www.nationalarchives.gov.uk/doc/open-government-licence/version/3).

Cover image © iStockphoto.com/FOTOKITA

The information in this book was believed to be correct at the time of writing. All content is for information purposes only and is not intended as legal advice. No liability is accepted by either the publisher or author for any errors or omissions (whether negligent or not) that it may contain. Professional advice should always be obtained before applying any information to particular circumstances.

Published 2019 by Law Brief Publishing, an imprint of Law Brief Publishing Ltd
30 The Parks
Minehead
Somerset
TA24 8BT

www.lawbriefpublishing.com

Paperback: 978-1-912687-22-0

For my mum who made me a feminist, my dad who made me argumentative.

For Rachel and Nathan who bring me joy and an escape from the bleakness every single day, and most of all to the women I represent who humble me with their bravery in the face of a system which does not seem to care about their safety.

And for Jimmy.

CONTENTS

Chapter One	Introduction	1
Chapter Two	What is Coercive Control?	5
Chapter Three	Why the Law Was Changed	17
Chapter Four	Coercive Control – The Law	35
Chapter Five	Issues With Charging and Sentencing Coercive Control	43
Chapter Six	Risk Assessment and How to Recognise a Victim of Coercive Control	57
Chapter Seven	Coercive Control and Legal Aid	61
Chapter Eight	Coercive Control and Family Law	71

CHAPTER ONE
INTRODUCTION

This is a book about coercive control from a legal perspective. I am a solicitor in private practice and the head of a specialist domestic abuse and stalking department dealing with cases all over England and Wales. I have specialised in this area for over 20 years and it is an area that I am passionate about.

I have been an advisor on the board of several refuges and domestic abuse services and volunteered my spare time within the services.

I am also the chair of Paladin, the National Stalking Advocacy Service and was heavily involved in the campaign which was the brain child of the Paladin founder, Laura Richards, to create a specific offence of coercive control as she saw that victims of coercive control were being failed by the criminal justice system leading to victims all too often ending up as homicide statistics. During this campaign we spoke to victims, members of the criminal justice system and the government about the gap in the law and the legislation we were proposing. Whilst the legislation was, as always, a compromise I do feel proud of what we achieved as, even though the legislation is not being utilised as often as it should be, it has helped many women and may well have prevented an escalation to homicide in some cases.

Even where women have not utilised the criminal justice system, they have told me how important it is that the coercive control law popularised the use of the term and started conversations throughout the country about this appalling crime. Many have told me that the term coercive control finally gave them the words to describe the psychological terrorism being inflicted on them.

I hope that it has also made perpetrators think about their behaviour and worry about being arrested and brought to justice.

I believe that it has also had more wide reaching effects other than simply providing a tool for the police to prosecute behaviours post December 2015.

It is a term now more widely used within the family courts and we have seen the successful appeal of Sally Challon represented by the fantastic Centre for Women's Justice. Sally had been a victim of coercive control by her husband for many decades before killing him in 2010 and was sentenced to life imprisonment for murder.

After coercive control was criminalised it allowed for a successful appeal by Sally to challenge the conviction for murder to one of manslaughter on the grounds of diminished responsibility due to the many years of coercive control she had been forced to endure. I very much hope this will be the first of many such cases.

Whilst this book is intended to be used by lawyers interested in coercive control and how this is relevant within the family law arena in particular, I also believe that it would be of use to other professionals working with victims of coercive control such as IDVAs, ISACs and ISVAs, refuge staff, social workers, Cafcass officers, housing officers, probation officers and magistrates.

I am of course aware that many victims who do not qualify for legal aid due to the narrow financial margins cannot afford legal representation and are forced to represent themselves against the man who has terrorised them for many years. Suddenly they are forced to face him in the family courts where he will continue to attempt to terrorise her and she is expected to formulate coherent arguments and present a legal case. I feel strongly that victims of domestic abuse, stalking and coercive control should receive legal aid to allow of representation in the family courts as of right. The legal aid should be non-means, non-merits so that a woman's financial circumstances are not relevant as is the case for parents facing care proceedings issued by the local authority. If the government is serious about tackling domestic abuse this is something that is vital in my view.

As I suspect that this may be some time off, I hope that this book will also be useful for victims who are forced to be litigants in person within family court proceedings so I have tried not to make this guide too technical.

I have attempted to include many of the tips and tactics I have amassed over the years in dealing with cases involving coercive control in the family courts. I have had to omit many other tactics as I feel that it would be counterproductive to publicly publish them as I am confident that perpetrators would use that knowledge against victims.

This guide is not intended to be a legal textbook as the legislation and case law is freely available online, the intention is to highlight issues around about coercive control in the family courts in particular and help victims to navigate their way through this process.

I should also briefly discuss the terminology used in this guide. I make no apologies for describing victims throughout this book as being female and perpetrators as being male. Whilst I fully accept that perpetrators can be female and victims can be male it is overwhelmingly the other way round in cases of domestic abuse and coercive control, which is expanded upon within this book, the sex bias being particularly dominant in coercive control and one of the components of it according to the man who coined the term Dr Evan Stark. Stark claims that "coercive control is used to secure male privilege and its regime of domination/subordination is constructed around the enforcement of gender stereotypes." It is also certainly borne out by my experience.

I also describe those accused of coercive control as "perpetrators" for ease of reference rather than as respondents, defendants, or alleged perpetrators and the same goes for victims but I accept that in many of the circumstances described in this guide the victim would be more properly described as a complainant or alleged victim.

This guide is based on over 20 years' experience of dealing with cases of coercive control throughout England and Wales on behalf of victims and therefore my experience is not restricted to any geographical area in particular. I also acknowledge that there is some great practice in the family courts where Judges go out of their way to achieve the right outcome and totally understand the dynamics of coercive control but unfortunately that is not the experience of most victims and I receive several desperate emails every day from victims recounting an all too similar experience of the family courts.

I do however still think that family court can achieve safety and protection for victims and their children but we cannot pretend that there does not need to be an overhaul of the system.

The law is correct as at up to the 30 August 2019.

Rachel Horman
September 2019

CHAPTER TWO
WHAT IS COERCIVE CONTROL?

This is the million dollar question and could be a very large book in itself. Many books have been written about what coercive control is so this chapter is only intended to give the reader a flavour of the nature of coercive control and I would urge you to read on about this elsewhere. Once you see coercive control you can't un-see it and you realise that it is far more common than you ever thought possible. You will read it in-between the lines of newspaper articles – usually about another woman murdered by her ex-partner. Some recent TV and radio programmes have done a good job in trying to demonstrate this form of abuse such as the Archers on Radio 4, although often the words coercive control are often never used.

Coercive control is not a new phenomenon – it has been around for thousands of years and yet it only became a criminal offence in 2015 in England and Wales.

Coercive control is, in my view, the essence of domestic abuse and is a targeted pattern of abuse against a partner. It is what allows a perpetrator to get away with terrorising his victim often for many years and seemingly often without the victim making concerted efforts to leave the relationship.

Coercive control includes many different types of abuse and may or may not include violence and sexual abuse. Coercive control is said to be one of the most dangerous types of abuse and a more reliable indicator of homicide than physical abuse which unfortunately is something that is still not understood by most agencies. It is often described as 'limiting a victim's space for action.'

Many perpetrators never need to utilise physical violence as the psychological terrorism that they inflict on their victim means that physical violence is simply not necessary, although physical violence may be utilised as a punishment for the victim's non-compliance. It is the fear caused by the coercive control, and the implicit threat of what will happen if she fails to comply, rather than the physical violence itself which makes victims feel unable to escape as the minutiae of their whole life and sanity is totally ruled by their perpetrator. Coercive control is designed to obtain the total submission of the victim to the perpetrator.

It may be the enforcement of petty rules and preferences of the perpetrator and the creation of a series of ever-changing "rules" in compliance of which the victim is forced to live her life. The victim can never fully know these rules as they are forever changing to suit the perpetrator and he may sometimes want her to break the rules on occasion so that he can remind her what the consequences are for breaking his rules and thereby increasing the fear and helplessness of the victim. The film "Sleeping with the Enemy" is often quoted to me by clients as being what it's like to live in a coercively controlling relationship with the petty requirements such as having to have the towels on the towel rail hanging totally level and all of the tins in the cupboard in groups with their labels facing to the front. This is not just someone suffering with a case of obsessive compulsive disorder, it is used to keep the victim controlled and there will be severe consequences for breach of these rules. Many clients tell me that they have to do excessive amounts of cleaning whilst the perpetrator is out so that she has no time for herself at all. This will then be checked by the perpetrator daily, and I've had dozens of clients tell me that the perpetrator will use a white glove to check for dust in hard to reach or remember places such as on the top of doors or on skirting boards. Clients tell me that their mobile phone is tracked by their partner so that he knows where she is, have their vaginas "checked" by the perpetrator when they return from the shops or visiting a family member to "check" whether they have had sexual relations with other men or women even when they have gone out with a child in a pram. I have had clients complain that their partner removes the fuses from the heating system when they go out so that they can't use it, timed when they go to the shops, locked into the house each time their partner leaves the house with even the windows locked. Behind all of this is the threat of, and often the use of, physical violence and rape, threats of physical violence and rape against the women's family, friends and children, threats to kill their children or have them removed by social services. The threats and violence are increased in intensity and frequency if the perpetrator thinks he is losing control in any way and particularly if he thinks she is preparing to leave.

Indeed separating from a coercively controlling partner is far and away the most dangerous time and the point at which women tend to be murdered by their partners.

Many liken coercive control to tactics to those used against prisoners of war – such as sleep deprivation, withholding food, drink and money, not being permitted to escape, constant questioning with punishment for the "wrong" answer, isolation, repetitive acts designed to cause fear, gaslighting and a destruction of the victim's own identity and belief system.

The term coercive control was popularised by Dr Evan Stark in his book Coercive Control, How Men Entrap Women in Personal Life [2007] although Dr Evan Stark does accept that the phrase was first used by unnamed feminist psychologists who described their abused clients as living in hostage-like situations.

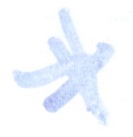

> *"Not only is coercive control the most common context in which [women] are abused, it is also the most dangerous"*
> – Evan Stark (2007) Coercive Control. How Men Entrap Women in Personal Life. New York: Oxford University Press.

Stark states that "coercive control targets a victim's autonomy, equality, liberty, social supports and dignity in ways that compromise the capacity for independent, self- interested, decision making, vital to escape and effective resistance to abuse. Coercive control often exploits and reinforces sexual inequalities in society which make it far more devastating for victims than when women are controlling".

Coercive control contains a myriad of different behaviours targeted to be most devastating and debilitating to that particular victim. Some describe it as domestic terrorism or akin to being stalked or held hostage in your own home during a relationship by the person who is supposed to love and care for you.

That person will know you better than anyone and will know all of your secrets, what scares you, what your phobias are, what you hold most dear and how to hurt you. That person may even be your carer and the perpetrator may be using the victim's disability against them or withholding care or medication.

Coercive control may include financial abuse, whereby a perpetrator withholds money from a victim totally, or allows them access to small pots of money which they then have to account to him for each penny, with consequences if she is unable to account fully or if he disagrees with what she spent money on, even though by rights the money actually belongs to her.

I have known several cases where victims have been forced to steal sanitary products or food for their children and rather than being treated as a victim are simply prosecuted as criminals without anyone asking why she was doing this.

Other victims may be financially controlled by being forced to take out debt on behalf of the perpetrator in their own name so that they are forced to spend all of their income on servicing the debt whilst the perpetrator retains access to all of "his" income in addition to the money she was forced to borrow. This means that often she would not be able to afford to rent anywhere on her own or even afford a train ticket to escape.

Coercive control is often the micro management of every aspect of your life including, in some cases, when you are allowed to go to the toilet. I have spoken to many clients who have been forced to ask permission to go to the toilet which is often refused forcing them to suffer the humiliation of having to wet themselves.

The Home Office published a Statutory Guidance Framework in relation to the new offence of coercive control which helpfully sets out the law and gives examples of the type of behaviour that might be used as a pattern of behaviour by a perpetrator but the guide makes it clear that the list is not exhaustive. As I said above, perpetrators will target what is held dear by a victim or what makes them vulnerable so each case will involve behaviour targeted specifically at that particular victim, and so it would be impossible to attempt to list all of the different examples of behaviour used against a victim of coercive control.

Gaslighting is a very common tactic used by a perpetrator of coercive control and involves the perpetrator repeatedly trying to convince the victim that they are wrong about something even when they aren't. It can lead to victims starting to believe that they are wrong and doubting their own sanity. Examples can include a perpetrator hiding her car keys and pretending that she must have left them in the fridge, turning off the oven so that she thinks she must have done it and forgotten, denying that they have said things or even had whole conversations.

Examples of coercive control given within the guidance framework for the law include:

- isolating a person from their friends and family;
- depriving them of their basic needs;
- monitoring their time;
- monitoring a person via online communication tools or using spyware;
- taking control over aspects of their everyday life, such as where they can go, who they can see, what to wear and when they can sleep;
- depriving them of access to support services, such as specialist support or medical services;
- repeatedly putting them down such as telling them they are worthless;
- enforcing rules and activity which humiliate, degrade or dehumanise the victim;
- forcing the victim to take part in criminal activity such as shoplifting,
- neglect or abuse of children to encourage self-blame and prevent disclosure to authorities;
- financial abuse including control of finances, such as only allowing a person a punitive allowance;

- threats to hurt or kill;
- threats to a child;
- threats to reveal or publish private information (e.g. threatening to 'out' someone).
- assault;
- criminal damage (such as destruction of household goods);
- rape;
- preventing a person from having access to transport or from working.
- monitoring someone online

Taken in isolation some of the examples may seem trivial however, taken as a whole with multiple examples day in day out, the behaviour becomes unbearable and has a devastating effect on the victim. Many victims of prolonged coercive control suffer with Post Traumatic Stress Disorder.

Imagine for a moment living in a relationship where a handful of the above tactics were being constantly employed against you. You might think that you wouldn't put up with it but coercive control will not be immediately apparent and happens by degree. Often a perpetrator will start by "love-bombing" a victim – also known as grooming. A victim will feel special and overwhelmed by love and devotion. He may "surprise" you by turning up unannounced so that you feel as though you can't say no and you then cancel your plans to be with others. This gives the perpetrator power as the victim starts to feel as though they can't imagine being without this wonderful person. Then the "drip, drip" starts with subtle criticisms – 'you look better in this... I miss you when I'm away from you – let's not go out with friends... your mum puts you down, I'm only defending you as I think you should be treated better by your friends and family... No one will love you like I do, why are you talking to him? I only get angry because I love you so much and can't stand the thought of losing you...' and so it begins.

Many victims – particularly young victims – confuse romance with coercive control. Being picked up from everywhere at the door by your partner might be romantic and considerate; or is it being done so that he knows where you are and so that you can't spend time with other men on the way home? Everyone likes to receive text messages from their partner especially in a new relationship but is he doing it to be romantic or because he wants to keep tabs on you. Is he asking you to send him a picture of the bar you are in because he's genuinely interested in its decor or because he wants proof you are where you say you are? The same behaviour can be acceptable in one relationship and tactics of abuse in another. The motivation of the behaviour is key, as are the consequences for failure to comply. By the time a victim realises what is happening it is usually too late and they are already deep into being coercively controlled and will find it difficult to get themselves out of it. Leaving may also lead to their death as the vast majority of women murdered by their partners are murdered on or shortly after separation. It is vital that agencies such as the police, social services, health and the family courts not only recognise this behaviour but are aware of the severe risks of it and the impact on the victim and children. It is also important that agencies ask the right questions so that they can help victims even if they themselves do not realise that they are victims. Most victims will not say that they are being coercively controlled whilst it is happening to them. It is only when they are out of it, and even then often only when they have had a domestic abuse support worker, that they will say the words "coercive control" so it is up to others to recognise this for them and call the behaviour what it is.

The guideline framework also emphasises the fact that whilst the legislation can be used against either sex coercive control is a "gendered" crime – i.e. that it is more likely to affect women as victims by male perpetrators than the other way around as women are disproportionately affected by domestic abuse.

It states: "In 2014/15, 92.4% of defendants in domestic abuse flagged cases were male. Where recorded, the proportion of female victims has remained steady at 84%, since 2010–11 (CPS Violence Against Women and Girls Crime Report 2014/15)."

The guidelines go on to explain that "Controlling or coercive behaviour is primarily a form of violence against women and girls and is underpinned by wider societal gender inequality. This can contribute to the ability of the offender to retain power and control, and ultimately the ability of the victim to access support and leave safely. It is, therefore, important to consider the role of gender in the context of power and control within a relationship when identifying controlling or coercive behaviour in heterosexual relationships." This is important as too often this point is missed or ignored leading to the "why doesn't she just leave" type of view which minimises the impact of coercive control and the inherent difficulties and risks in leaving.

Coercive control is a repeat crime as domestic abuse is a pattern of behaviour rather than a one off incident between two adults. The fact that women are overwhelmingly its prime victims is found in study after study and is certainly backed up by my own professional experience. 89% of all those who had experienced 4 or more incidents of domestic violence were women (Domestic violence, sexual assault and stalking: Findings from the British Crime Survey, Sylvia Walby and Jonathan Allen, 2004).

The charity Refuge remind us that:

"The intensity and severity of violence used by men is more extreme, with men being more likely to use physical violence, threats, and harassment"
– (Hester, M. Who Does What to Whom? Gender and Domestic Violence Perpetrators, 2009)

Although 1 in 6 men report experiencing violence from a female partner or ex-partner each year, women are:

- 4 times as likely to experience the most serious and potentially lethal violence, such as threats, assault with a gun or knife, choking and sexual assault

- 3 times more likely to report suffering a physical injury

- Twice as likely to report chronic on going assaults, defined as more than 10 separate incidents

- 5 times as likely to report that they feared for their lives

(Jaffe, P.G, Lemon N.K.D, Poisson, S.E, 2003)

In a significant majority of cases where a man reports abuse, he has also perpetrated violence towards his partner (Final report of the ad-hoc Federal-Provincial-Territorial Working Group reviewing spousal abuse policies and legislation. Canada, 2003).

Men are less likely to have been repeat victims of domestic assault, less likely to be seriously injured and less likely to report feeling fearful in their own homes (Scottish Executive Central Research Unit, 2002).

This is why I make no apology for referring in this publication to women being victims and men being perpetrators and if you think that this chapter sounds extreme or like a film script think again –

these examples are what fills my day, and those of my department, every single day of the week.

victims are then referred to **Multi Agency Risk Assessment Conferences** (MARACS) to share information about victims, discuss their safety and come up with a safely plan. MARACS were first set up in 2003 on the premise that no one agency has the whole picture of a victim's experiences and no one agency alone can solve the issue. They are attended by agencies such as police, social services, housing, health, probation, refuge, drug and alcohol services etc. whilst the victim is not present but her views are represented by an **Independent Domestic Violence Advocate** (IDVA) who will feed back to the victim after the meeting. IDVAs work with high risk victims of domestic abuse and advocate on their behalf with agencies. They often attend court with clients. In addition to IDVAs there are now also Independent Sexual Violence Advocates (ISVAs), Independent Stalking Advocate Caseworkers) and KIDVAs who work with young people. I have found these advocates to be invaluable in providing practical assistance to clients around issues such as housing and support within the criminal justice system which is essential if a client is to be successful in leaving her partner.

The DASH is more than a risk assessment tool in my view – it is an excellent tool to get information from victims – it is a conversation starter rather than a tick box exercise and ensures that we are asking the right questions when we come into contact with victims as victims will not necessarily volunteer information but often say to me "why didn't they ask me?" It is a tool that my team use on a daily basis to ensure that we are obtaining a full picture from clients.

Domestic Violence Homicide Reviews were established on a statutory footing in 2004 with the Domestic Violence, Crime and Victims Act to focus on learning lessons from failures which may have contributed to the homicide of domestic abuse victims aged 16 and over in the same way that there were reviews taking place for children who were murdered by family members. They are meant to inform change to national policies and procedures and highlight good practice to make the future safer for victims. Some are better than others and a strong chair who does not have links to the agencies in the room as well as ensuring that the right people are in the room such as GPs is vital in my view. I would also like to see agencies being held accountable instead of just hearing the oft-repeated disingenuous apology of "lessons will be learned". Unfortunately they never are.

The Family Law Act (FLA) was introduced in 1996 which brought improved protection for victims in the family court and whilst "molestation" was deliberately not defined case law has made it was clear that the notion of "molestation" was not restricted to physical violence. The FLA allows for orders to prohibit communication – both on and off line, intimidation, threats or harassment, amongst other things. It also allows for occupation orders which can force out a perpetrator of abuse from the family home even if it is held in his sole name and the parties are not married. S1 of the **Domestic Violence, Crime and Victims Act 2004** amended the FLA to make breach of a non-molestation order a criminal offence with a maximum sentence of 5 years imprisonment rather than the 2 year maximum under the previous Contempt of Court provisions.

Forced Marriage Protection Orders

These civil orders came into effect in 2008 in the Forced Marriage (Civil Protection) Act 2007 with intention of preventing a forced marriage from taking place or to protect the victim of one if she leaves a forced marriage. "Force" includes coercion and emotional blackmail so there is no requirement for it to be physical and this force may come from more than one family member – often including extended family not even in the country. This "force" can include behaviour such as a parent telling their daughter that if she doesn't go through with the marriage of their choice her grandmother will have a heart attack with the stress and shame. This places a huge burden on a young person and negates the possibility of full and "free consent" and is often part of a coercively controlling relationship.

These orders can impose restrictions on various people - often multiple respondents from certain types of behaviour e.g. threats of violence, intimidation, harassment, making arrangements for any marriage or engagement, making arrangements for the victim to travel abroad, and routinely order the surrender of the victim's passports on the basis that they be retained by the court or her solicitor.

Orders are often made in the High Court as only the High Court can detain foreign passports and its orders are more likely to be enforced abroad. Given the "specialist nature" (MOJ forced marriage guidance and information document) only 15 County Courts including the principal registry are approved to make these orders to ensure that the applications are dealt with by Judges with experience in this type of honour-based violence. The Forced Marriage Unit talk about the "one-chance rule" with forced marriage cases which underlies how seriously they treat these cases.

Interestingly, orders can be made by third parties rather than just the victim e.g. police, teachers or social services without the consent of the victim.

Orders protect the victim at any age and in 2011 the Forced Marriage Unit says it deals with cases of victims aged from 5 to 87 years old.

Initially it was not a criminal offence to breach a forced marriage protection order even though it had been a criminal offence to breach a non-molestation order since 2007 – I believe that this was in part a misguided political correctness which failed to put the protection of victims first. This situation changed on 16 June 2014 and breach of a forced marriage protection order is now a criminal offence with the maximum penalty 5 Years imprisonment. This brought the legislation into line with breach of non-molestation orders.

Criminal offence of forced marriage

Forced marriage in itself, however, was still not a criminal offence and did not become one until 16 June 2014 with the Anti-social Behaviour, Crime and Policing Act.

This created two criminal offences:

1. forced marriage in its own right and
2. breaching a civil forced marriage protection order.

A perpetrator is guilty of forced marriage if he:

1. uses violence, threats or any form of coercion for the purpose of causing another person to enter into a marriage and
2. believes, or ought reasonably to believe, that the conduct may cause the other person to enter into the marriage without free and full consent.

This Act makes reference to "coercion" long before the coercive control legislation was passed.

If the victim lacks mental capacity to marry then there is no need to show violence, threats or coercion. The law has been drafted to make it a criminal offence for forced marriage to take place outside the UK which is essential for this particular crime. It should however be remembered that not all forced marriages take place abroad and that they also often happen in the UK.

The law defines a marriage as a civil or religious ceremony which is important and the Act states that the conduct of the perpetrator may be directed at the victim or another person. This would therefore cover a perpetrator making threats to, or assaulting the victim's mother if the victim didn't agree to the marriage for example.

The maximum sentence is 7 years imprisonment and there could be other charges brought in addition to forced marriage such as coercive control.

The numbers of prosecutions for this offence is disappointingly low. The response to a Freedom of Information request submitted to Lancashire Constabulary in February 2015 was that after 6 months of the legislation there had not been anyone charged in Lancashire with the offence, even though my firm were dealing with lots of forced marriage protection orders in Lancashire and beyond. Why was this? Police training is an issue, being aware that it is a crime and not just "part of their religion" and understanding the difference between forced and arranged marriages. Also, I believe that too much emphasis is put on the victim's wishes in a way that doesn't happen with other crimes apart from domestic abuse and sexual assault. It is not the victims responsibility to decide whether or not there should be a prosecution. The government have made it a criminal offence so the police should act upon it. This is a view also shared by Karma Nirvana, the charity who support victims of honour-based abuse and forced marriage. I understand that there are additional issues that would affect a victim of this crime as she may be shunned from her family and community in some cases, however, when we consider that rape and sexual assault usually flow from a forced marriage we need to have a more robust response, whilst also putting in more resources to support victims through this process. The publicity around the handful of successful prosecutions will also eventually contribute to a reduction of this hideous crime.

Claire's Law – formally known as the domestic violence disclosure scheme

This scheme came into force on 8 March 2014 on International Women's Day – after a 12 month pilot scheme in Manchester, Gwent, Nottinghamshire and Wiltshire.

It was also pushed along by a campaign by the family of Clare Wood, who was murdered in 2009 by her ex-boyfriend George Appleton. Clare had met Appleton over the internet and she was unaware of his violent history of violence towards ex-girlfriends, including abducting a previous girlfriend at knifepoint. She was stalked by him after separation and he eventually raped her, strangled her to death and then set fire to her body. Her family believe that had this been in place at the time she may have been saved.

The scheme allows the police to disclose to individuals details of their partners' abusive pasts however it should be noted that the scheme did not introduce any new legislation. The scheme is based on the police's common law power to disclose information where it is necessary to prevent crime. The scheme provides a processes for the exercise of the powers.

It is not restricted to criminal convictions but to information held by the police.

It should be pointed out that currently the scheme does not create a "right to know." The application can't just be made by anyone and the applicant has to demonstrate that the information is necessary

Right to review scheme

The scheme only applies to cases after 5 June 2013 and comes from the case of R v Christopher Killick [2011] which gave the victim of a crime (and their family if deceased) the right to request a review of a CPS decision not to prosecute or to discontinue proceedings or to allow to "lie on the file" as in the case of Jane Clough whose parents always say that perversely the best way to get away with rape is to murder the victim.

If you qualify for "enhanced entitlements" you may request a face to face review at the conclusion of the review to discuss the decision.

Enhanced entitlements include – victims of the most serious crime, persistently targeted victims, vulnerable or intimidated victims.

The procedure is that a victim should contact the decision making CPS office (by email) within 5 working days of the decision being communicated to them as that within that timescale there is more likelihood of recommencement of proceedings. The maximum time limit is said to be 3 months unless there are exceptional circumstances.

Cinderella Law

This was enacted by the Serious Crime Bill which received Royal Assent in March 2015.

It clarifies the offence of child cruelty in s1 of the Children and Young Persons Act 1933 to include psychological suffering or injury as well as physical harm.

It must be wilful and likely to cause unnecessary suffering or injury to health.

The maximum penalty continues to be 10 years in custody.

Practice Direction 12J

PD12J, as it is known, was originally issued in 20018 and refers to cases in the family courts where it is alleged that domestic abuse has been perpetrated and it sets down how the family courts should deal with such cases. It advocates the use of finding of fact hearings so that the court can make findings about the allegations of domestic abuse. Unfortunately, there are still many claims that this is not being followed by the family courts. This is covered in more detail later on in the book.

Yet, notwithstanding all of the above improvements, many people were surprised to learn that was no actual criminal offence of domestic abuse. Instead the police and CPS had to utilise laws which were not designed for domestic abuse, many of which were created over 150 years ago and designed for cases of men being violent to other men away from the home.

Types of offences used

- Common assault – Offences against the person Act 1861 (OAPA 1861)

- Actual bodily harm – Offences against the person Act 1861 (OAPA 1861)

- Grievous bodily harm – Offences against the person Act 1861 (OAPA 1861)

(a) A has responsibility for B, for the purposes of Part 1 of the Children and Young Persons Act 1933 (see section 17 of that Act), and

(b) B is under 16.

*(4) A's behaviour has a "**serious effect**" on B if—*

(a) it causes B to fear, on at least two occasions, that violence will be used against B, or

(b) it causes B serious alarm or distress which has a substantial adverse effect on B's usual day-to-day activities.

*(5) For the purposes of subsection (1)(d) A "**ought to know**" is defined as that which a reasonable person in possession of the same information would know.*

(6) For the purposes of subsection (2)(b)(i) A and B are members of the same family if—

(a) they are, or have been, married to each other;

(b) they are, or have been, civil partners of each other;

(c) they are relatives;

(d) they have agreed to marry one another (whether or not the agreement has been terminated);

(e) they have entered into a civil partnership agreement (whether or not the agreement has been terminated);

(f) they are both parents of the same child;

(g) they have, or have had, parental responsibility for the same child.

(7) In subsection (6)—

- *"civil partnership agreement" has the meaning given by section 73 of the Civil Partnership Act 2004;*

- *"child" means a person under the age of 18 years;*

- *"parental responsibility" has the same meaning as in the Children Act 1989;*

- *"relative" has the meaning given by section 63(1) of the Family Law Act 1996.*

(8) In proceedings for an offence under this section it is a defence for A to show that—

(a) in engaging in the behaviour in question, A believed that he or she was acting in B's best interests, and

(b) the behaviour was in all the circumstances reasonable.

(9) A is to be taken to have shown the facts mentioned in subsection (8) if—

(a) sufficient evidence of the facts is adduced to raise an issue with respect to them, and

(b) the contrary is not proved beyond reasonable doubt.

(10) The defence in subsection (8) is not available to A in relation to behaviour that causes B to fear that violence will be used against B.

(11) A person guilty of an offence under this section is liable—

(a) on conviction on indictment, to imprisonment for a term not exceeding five years, or a fine, or both;

(b) on summary conviction, to imprisonment for a term not exceeding 12 months, or a fine, or both.

It should be noted there is a requirement for the parties to be in a current relationship unless they are still residing together. This point is often missed which is why I highlighted the word **and** at para 76(2)(b)

Paragraph 76(4)(b) is drafted in the same way as S4a of the stalking legislation (Protection from Harassment Act 1997 as amended by the Protection of Freedoms Act 2012) which makes it an offence to pursue a course of conduct which causes "serious alarm or distress" which has a substantial adverse effect on the day-to-day activities of the victim. This limb of the legislation was campaigned for by Laura Richards, the Paladin founder, to demonstrate the overall emotional and psychological harm that stalking causes to victims, even where an explicit fear of violence is not created by each incident of stalking behaviour. The same applies to the coercive control situation and the legislation reflects that there is no need for there to be a threat.

The phrase 'substantial adverse effect on B's usual day-to-day activities' may include many examples of behaviour but it is clear that it includes but is not limited to:

- Stopping or changing the way someone socialises

- Physical or mental health deterioration

- A change in routine at home including those associated with mealtimes or household chores

- Attendance record at school

- Putting in place measures at home to safeguard themselves or their children

- Changes to work patterns, employment status or routes to work

It is important that victims consider how the behaviour has impacted them during the course of the relationship, as it is relevant to the legislation and, without showing serious alarm or distress which has a substantial adverse impact, the victim will need to show that they fear that violence will be used.

The emergence of defence available under the legislation was disappointing as we feared that it would be commonly used by perpetrators to say that the abuse was "in her best interests". This is often claimed be perpetrators particularly in relation to financial abuse where they will claim that the victim is not fit to look after money. I am pleased that an objective element was added to the defence that requires that the "behaviour was in all the circumstances reasonable".

The maximum sentence is 5 years imprisonment however I feel that there is scope for this to be increased now in view of the successful campaign to increase the sentence for stalking (on which the coercive control legislation is based) to a maximum of 10 years. As the examples of behaviour in cases of stalking and coercive control are often interchangeable it does seem an anomaly now to have this differential.

CHAPTER FIVE
ISSUES WITH CHARGING AND SENTENCING COERCIVE CONTROL

I want to examine in more detail some of the reasons or excuses given as to why coercive control is not prosecuted very often as I do not believe that most of them stand up to scrutiny. I also hope that this chapter will also assist in advocating on behalf of victims with the police and crown prosecution service, for example by utilising the victims right to review scheme. Many of the points regarding gathering of evidence for criminal prosecutions are also pertinent to the preparation in family cases for a finding of fact hearing or contested non-molestation order.

The Coercive control legislation is still vastly underutilised by the police and the Crown Prosecution Service in dealing with domestic abuse cases, and more often than not, when you see a case where charges of coercive control have been brought there is also an assault which features in the behaviour yet is not charged separately.

When we campaigned for the creation of the criminal offence of coercive control it was anticipated that the law would be used in addition to existing laws where possible such as assault, however, sadly this often is not the case.

In December 2018 the BBC reported that in the first 2.5 years of the law being in force there were only 7034 arrests and, of this, only 1157 cases where the suspect was actually charged, with just 235 successful convictions since the law came into effect.

In my view this highlights issues not only with the police but also with the CPS recognising this offence as all too often incidents are dealt with in isolation rather than joining them together to highlight a pattern of behaviour which would enable a charge of coercive control.

Instead, too often charges are brought in relation to criminal damage or an assault, with the more serious but low-level ongoing psychological abuse ignored and not charged, when in fact it is this behaviour that is the causing the most injury to the victim and presents most risk to them.

It is the drip, drip effect of the constant coercive control that victims want recognised as an offence rather than the perpetrator being punished for smashing her car window, which does not signify the reality of what has been happening to her.

It is particularly important that coercive control is recognised and offenders are punished for the offence, not only because of the high risk of significant harm and/or homicide but also because the abuse often involves the gaslighting of the victim so that they believe that no one will believe them or that the psychological terrorism is not happening or is their fault. A successful conviction of coercive control goes some way to rebalancing this.

It is also important in my view to document what has happened in a legal sense and to hold perpetrators to account. A criminal record for criminal damage tells a very different story to a criminal record for coercive control and should be a red flag to agencies such as social services, the family court and future partners in a way that a conviction for criminal damage would not be.

We need to ensure that our frontline police officers and the CPS are properly trained in relation to coercive control and that resources are available to allow for proper investigations to take place in relation to this offence. It is much quicker to investigate and charge in relation to an assault where there is an obvious physical injury. Obtaining evidence in relation to an allegation of coercive control will often take longer but this should not prevent it from happening.

The statutory guidance framework is a really useful document and attempts to demonstrate the nature of coercive control to some extent and make it clear to the police and other agencies that perpetrators may seek to exploit the vulnerabilities of victims in order to maintain control and prevent them from obtaining help. Examples are given including:

1. Impairment of physical and mental health issues – in practice I see victims' mental health being used against them on a regular basis by the perpetrator and being seen as an excuse by the police not to investigate particularly if the "best interests" defence is raised. If you have lived with many years of coercive control then it is likely that you will suffer with some form of mental health issue.

2. Ethnicity and immigration status are highlighted as issues which may make obtaining help more difficult, however, I still see the police using the alleged perpetrator to interpret on behalf of the victim which should never happen.

3. Children being used against the victim so that they believe that the children will be removed if they report abuse.

4. Financial abuse – this is a very common tactic by abusers but can make it extremely difficult for women to leave if they do not even have money to buy sanitary products or bus fare. It does however often provide evidence for the police to use in the form of bank statements. There is a proposal within the

domestic abuse bill to make this a specific criminal offence, however without proper training I fear that, just like the coercive control legislation, this too would be under utilised.

5. Drugs and alcohol – Perpetrators may have encouraged or forced the victim to become dependent on these substances or victims may have used them as a coping mechanism in the face of the psychological terrorism they are being exposed to. Either way, if your perpetrator controls your supply this creates additionally difficulties in leaving. Victims may also be fearful that their substance misuse will be publicised by the perpetrator to the police and or social services. In my experience victims with substance misuse issues receive a worse service from the agencies who are there to help them than women without these issues.

6. Homosexuality – threats to "out "the victim to family or work colleagues if they leave or report the abuse.

7. Forced marriage and so called "honour" based abuse - Whilst there is specific legislation available for victims of forced marriage these victims may be more reluctant to leave a coercively controlling relationship due to the reaction of their family or community.

8. Age – an older person may be more reliant upon their abuser for their care or financial support.

The guidelines also cover the police investigation of coercive control and emphasise the fact that victims may not recognise themselves as victims and states that the police consider this new offence in all callouts.

It recommends that officers "ask questions about rules, decision-making, norms and fear in the relationship rather than what has just happened" in relation to the incident they are called out to and to consider the wider context. If the police adhered to this advice and the advice to investigate the prosecution and conviction rate would, in my view, be significantly higher.

The guidance also advises that, where a physical assault has taken place, coercive control may also be present which can be charged in addition to other offences.

There is also a useful section in relation to tactics often employed by perpetrators such as making false allegations against the victim. In the authorised professional practice on investigating domestic abuse issued by the College of policing it states "a manipulative perpetrator may be trying to draw the police into colluding with their coercive control of the victim. Police officers must avoid playing into the primary perpetrators hands and take account of all available evidence when making the decision to arrest." This is an extremely common tactic in my view and something which often is not recognised by the police who are too quick to jump to the "six of one and half a dozen of the other" position without looking at the wider context and identifying the actual victim.

Many officers will complain that obtaining evidence of coercive control is too difficult and this is why prosecutions are rare. I believe that the truth is more likely that the police often do not invest the time to carry out a proper investigation and that in many cases there is readily available evidence. It is something that I look at with clients in relation to family or civil applications and victims often tell me that the police have not been interested when they previously told them about this evidence which I go on to use successfully in court.

The guidelines list types of evidence which could be useful in relation to prosecutions but again is at pains to point out that this list is not exhaustive. Examples of evidence include:

- copies of emails;

- phone records;

- text messages;

- evidence of abuse over the internet, digital technology and social media platforms;

- evidence of an assault;

- photographs of injuries such as: defensive injuries to forearms, latent upper arm grabs, scalp bruising, clumps of hair missing;

- 999 tapes or transcripts;

- CCTV;

- body worn video footage;

- lifestyle and household including at scene photographic evidence;

- records of interaction with services such as support services, (even if parts of those records relate to events which occurred before the new offence came into force, their contents may still, in certain circumstances, be relied on in evidence);

- medical records;

- witness testimony, for example the family and friends of the victim may be able to give evidence about the effect and impact of isolation of the victim from them;

- local enquiries: neighbours, regular deliveries, postal, milk delivery, window cleaner etc;

- bank records to show financial control;

- previous threats made to children or other family members;

- diary kept by the victim;

- victims account of what happened to the police, however this is not the only evidence that can be used to prove a case;

- evidence of isolation such as lack of contact between family and friends, victim withdrawing from activities such as clubs, perpetrator accompanying victim to medical appointments;

- house-to-house enquiries;

- automatic number plate recognition;

- covert surveillance;

- information from other agencies such as housing association records showing recurrent damage such as holes in walls or complaints from other tenants or school records noting restrictions on collection of children from the school by one of the parents.

The guidance also makes it clear that the job of building the case for the victim and gathering the evidence is for the police rather than the victim however in reality this is not the case and I regularly assist victims in compiling relevant evidence for the police or for use in the victims right to review scheme

The guidance warns that there may be reasons why victims will indicate that they do not wish to proceed and this should not mean that the case will automatically be stopped. In my experience where victims are supported throughout the criminal justice system and victims believe that the police are doing all that they can to help it gives them confidence in the system and they are far less likely to withdraw co-operation for the prosecution. In addition to this the responsibility or decision to prosecute should not be on victims - if a criminal offence has been committed then it should be prosecuted. If perpetrators believe that by intimidating the victim sufficiently to withdraw their cooperation the prosecution is likely to stop then of course this is exactly what they will do. I have spoken to many victims in the circumstances who have said that they were secretly glad that the prosecution continued after they had attempted to withdraw their statement as they did not feel "responsible" for what happened to the perpetrator and therefore felt that he was less likely to seek revenge.

The CPS (2013) directors guidance on charging, fifth edition specifies that all domestic abuse cases must be charged by the CPS and would obviously include coercive control cases.

This means that victims have to rely on the relevant CPS lawyer also understanding coercive control and the dynamics of domestic abuse. The Victims Right to Review scheme does, however, provide victims with an appeals process in the event that they feel that the incorrect decision has been made with regard to charging the perpetrator. Victims can use the scheme for decisions made after 5 June 2013 after the case of R v Christopher Killick [2001] where the decision has been made not to charge at all or in cases where the victim believes that the incorrect charge has been brought against the perpetrator. It can also be used in cases where a decision has been made to discontinue proceedings or offer no evidence.

The Victims Code states that the scheme even applies to relatives or partners in homicide cases and provides for enhanced entitlements for certain victims including "persistently targeted "or "vulnerable or intimidated victims" Many victims of coercive control are likely to fall into this category commonly through the "intimidated witness" provision which will also entitle the victim to special measures at court.

Victims are supposed to be informed in a letter detailing the reasons why a decision not to prosecute has been made and about the right to seek a review of the decision however, in my experience, this often does not happen.

I am often asked to assist victims in preparing a letter for the victims right to review scheme and the guidelines state that a request for a review should be made within five working days from the date of the communication of the decision which does not allow the victim much time to process the information and seek legal advice if required.

Requests can be made out of this timeframe and up to 3 months from the communication of the decision however the CPS states that a delayed request may decrease the chances of (re) commencing proceedings as the scheme has to also take into account the fairness on the alleged perpetrator. Only in exceptional cases will a request be considered outside of the three-month limit.

The initial local resolution stage of the scheme is checked by a prosecutor who has not been involved in the original decision and they promise a "clear and detailed explanation of the decision".

There are three possible outcomes to this stage:

1. They agree the decision was wrong and if they are unable to (re) commence proceedings will apologise

2. Decide the original decision was right but provide more of an explanation

3. Decide the original decision was right and there is no more information to be provided

The above should normally be completed within 10 days of receipt of the victims right to review request. If a victim is not happy with the decision at the local resolution stage she can request an independent review.

An Independent review is a reconsideration of the evidence and public interest test undertaken by a reviewing prosecutor independent of the original decision who is supposed to approach the case afresh.

Victims entitled to enhanced assistant under the victims code will be offered a face-to-face meeting to discuss the outcome of this stage. The independent review should, where possible, be completed and the outcome communicated to the victim within 6 weeks.

This is a useful tool and can result in charges being brought where the initial decision was made not to charge for any offence at all.

It is vital that victims of coercive control are kept informed with regard to the criminal justice process and that they are adequately protected in the run up to trial, ideally by the perpetrator being held on remand or by robust bail conditions being in place. Unfortunately this does not always happen and I have seen cases of perpetrators being bailed to live a few doors down from the victim so that she has to see him every day intimidating her by his presence. Other cases I have dealt with include bail conditions being removed altogether after the perpetrator is taken back to court in relation to a breach of the bail conditions. Many victims who feel that the bail conditions are not adequately protecting them should consult a solicitor who will be able to obtain a non-molestation order for them offering more comprehensive protection. Whilst this should not be necessary, in reality, victims are often forced to do this in order to feel safe.

Sentencing coercive control

Whilst coercive control became a criminal offence in December 2015 it was not until the 1st of October 2018 that the sentencing council published sentencing guidelines with regard to this offence.

In my experience coercive control has not been sentenced in a sufficiently robust way when you consider that the maximum sentence available for each offence of coercive control is five years imprisonment.

It could also be argued that the sentence in relation to coercive control should be increased in line with stalking to 10 years on the basis that the coercive control legislation was drafted along the same lines as the stalking legislation as the behaviours and impact were seen as almost identical just at different points on a time line. Coercive control taking place during a relationship whilst the same behaviours after separation are then classified under the criminal law as stalking rather than coercive control. Paladin campaigned with Dr Eleanor Aston, who had been stalked on numerous occasions by Raymond Knight, a former patient, who would immediately resume his chilling behaviour towards her upon release from short prison sentences.

The judge, sentencing Knight for a second time, described Knight as dangerous and expressed frustration that he was limited to a five year sentence.

The law was changed in 2017 increasing the term for section 4A from 5 to 10 years and from 7 to 14 years for racially or religiously aggravated harassment. Unfortunately coercive control was not included within the policing and crime bill which I believe was a mistake.

In relation to sentencing coercive control the factors set out by the sentencing council to demonstrate higher culpability in relation to the offence include:

- Conduct intended to maximise fear or distress

- Persistent action over a prolonged period

- Use of multiple methods of controlling or coercive behaviour

- Sophisticated offence

- Conduct intended to humiliate and degrade the victim

When the Judge assesses harm caused by coercive control the factors to be taken into account in relation to a category two Level include fear of violence on at least two occasions and serious alarm or distress which has caused a substantial adverse effect on the victim.

Category one level of harm would include fear of violence on many occasions, very serious alarm or distress which has a substantial adverse effect on the victim and significant psychological harm.

Factors to be taken into account to increase the seriousness of an offence in addition to the statutory aggravating factors such as previous convictions, offences committed in a UK and hate crimes are:

1. Steps taken to prevent the victim reporting an incident

2. Steps taken to prevent the victim obtaining assistance

3. A proven history of violence or threats by the offender in a domestic context

4. Impact of offence on others particularly children

5. Exploiting contact arrangements with a child to commit the offence

6. Victim is particularly vulnerable (not all vulnerabilities are immediately apparent)

7. Victim left in debt, destitute or homeless

8. Failure to comply with current court orders

9. Offence committed on license or post sentence supervision

10. Offences taken into consideration

Many of these factors are very common in most coercive control cases.

Factors which would reduce seriousness or reflect personal mitigation:

1. No previous convictions or no relevance/recent convictions

2. Remorse

3. Good character and/or exemplary conduct paragraph serious medical condition requiring urgent, intensive or long-term treatment

4. Age and/or lack of maturity

5. Mental disorder or a learning disability

6. Sole or primary care area for dependent relatives

7. Determination and/or demonstration of steps having been taken to address offending behaviour

In addition to the police and CPS prosecutors who would benefit from more training in relation to the dynamics and impact of coercive control Judges, magistrates and probation officers should be added to that list as the criminal courts regularly minimise the impact and risk associated with coercive control. Until this happens sentences will fail to protect victims adequately in my view and perpetrators will continue in their behaviour.

Postscript – up until very recently it was not possible for victims of coercive control to challenge the sentences passed down by the courts but in September 2019 the government announced that 14 offences, including coercive control and stalking; were being added to the unduly lenient sentence scheme which looks at sentences where they are deemed to be too low. These can be reviewed by the Attorney General's office and, if appropriate, referred to the court of appeal so I hope that this will be utilised by victims and the public in the future.

CHAPTER SIX
RISK ASSESSMENT AND HOW TO RECOGNISE A VICTIM OF COERCIVE CONTROL

While some victims will be aware of the term "coercive control" and understand its definition the majority of victims will not. Usually the ones that recognise and identify themselves with the term have separated from their partner some time ago, allowing them distance and the ability to make sense of what has happened to them, often with the assistance of a domestic abuse advocate. The vast majority of victims, and in particular the ones who are still in the relationship or have just left the relationship, are unlikely to use the term or even necessarily see themselves as victims of domestic abuse or coercive control. This chapter will hopefully help professionals to understand the importance of the risk assessment process and start to use one with victims which may well save lives.

Often a client will come into my office about one thing – perhaps a divorce or a financial agreement heavily weighted in favour of their ex-partner and leave with a non-molestation order or advice to reconsider their position around the children or finances due to safeguarding considerations which have come from ascertaining that this is a coercive control case. Victims leaving an abusive relationships are certainly not in a position to make informed and free decisions regarding financial settlements and all too often they are agreeing to give up entitlements to many hundreds of thousands of pounds simply "for an easy life" which usually translates to fear of the perpetrator.

The job of a professional in the circumstances whether it be a solicitor, a social worker, a Cafcass officer or a police officer is to ask the right questions to rule out the possibility of abuse and coercive control. It may seem excessive to do this with every client even if they haven't mentioned it but when one considers that at least one in four women will experience domestic abuse it would be negligent, in my view, not to.

So how can we best obtain this information and get a full picture from the client?

In my experience the best tool in order to do this is the DASH risk assessment.

I do not use the risk assessment to count the ticks in the boxes and refer to a Marac although this may also be the outcome. The main purpose of using the assessment is to obtain the correct information and start a conversation.

The DASH risk assessment was created by Laura Richards in partnership with Safe Lives (formerly CAADA) and was based on research about the indicators of high risk of domestic abuse.

Some have criticised the DASH for not having a section on coercive control but whilst the questions do not use the phrase "coercive control" more than half of the questions within the checklist do relate to coercive control type situations. This is intentional. If you ask a woman if she has been subjected to coercive control, more than likely she will not know what you mean and say no.

If you ask more specific examples about controlling behaviour then you are more likely to obtain relevant information as she recognises these examples as happening in her own life. Similarly if you ask a victim if she has ever been raped by her husband most will say no. If you rephrase the question to ask whether she has ever been forced or pressurised to have sexual intercourse against her will often the answer will more likely be yes. The DASH asks whether the perpetrator does things of a sexual nature which makes her feel bad. This opens up the discussion far wider, allowing for disclosure around sexual assault and threats to disclose sexual images etc. Unfortunately, many victims still do not see the actions of their perpetrators as being criminal offences, which is actually how the law and the police have seen things but it is also due to brainwashing and gaslighting from the perpetrator. Domestic abuse was perfectly legal in the past – in a case in 1782 Judge Buller reportedly stated that a man was permitted to beat his wife so long as the rod he used was "no thicker than his thumb." In 1895 a London byelaw was passed to prevent men beating their wives between the hours of 10pm and 7am as the noise was stopping people from sleeping. More recently, it was only in 1976 that the Domestic Violence and matrimonial Proceedings Act was passed as the first law to offer protection from domestic violence to victims, with rape within marriage only being clarified as a criminal offence in 1991.

When this is then compounded by a reluctance by the police to take these crimes seriously it is hardly surprising that women don't perceive what is happening to them as illegal or that what is happening to them isn't normal. It is the duty of the professional to get this information from victims and the excuse of "she never said" just is not good enough.

CHAPTER SEVEN
COERCIVE CONTROL AND LEGAL AID

This chapter is designed to help the practitioners, victims or victims' advocates understand the rules around eligibility for legal aid in family law cases – not in relation to financial eligibility which can be assessed with the online calculator – but with regard to the updated rules requiring that victims evidence that they are a victim of domestic abuse in order to obtain legal aid for children or financial proceedings. There is no requirement for domestic abuse evidence in order to get legal aid for a non-molestation order or other protective order.

As a result of the 2012 Legal Aid, Sentencing and Punishment of Offenders Act (Laspo), from 1 April 2013 Legal Aid was removed from most areas of family law unless the client could evidence that she had been a victim of "domestic violence" (s33 The Civil Legal Aid (Procedure) Regulations 2012).

Over the years the list of acceptable evidence has expanded and the time limit on how long ago the abuse occurred has been removed (largely due to a much needed judicial review by Rights of Women). There is scope within most of the evidential options to utilise coercive control rather than simply physical violence to fulfil the evidential requirements.

The list of acceptable evidence (known as domestic violence gateway evidence) for legal aid purposes is shown below. There is also a separate list outside the scope of this book in relation to child abuse. Reference is made to "associated persons" as in the Family law Act 1996 definition. For some types of evidence the evidence may relate to another person "associated" to the perpetrator such as his ex-girlfriend and it does not need to be in relation to the client if she is also "associated" to the perpetrator – this is referred to below as "third party evidence".

Schedule 1 (para 1) Arrest for a relevant domestic violence offence

The list of domestic violence offences is too long to list here and can be found on the Ministry of Justice website. The list includes coercive control but there are many other offences which could also be used to prosecute discrete elements of some coercive control behaviour such as blackmail, criminal damage, assault, sexual assault, child abduction, harassment, stalking, malicious communications, breach of a non-molestation order and false imprisonment. The list is already out of date in relation to many other domestic abuse type offences such as disclosing private sexual photographs or films without consent. This section of evidence only requires the perpetrator to have been arrested in relation to one of these offences and for there to be an ongoing investigation. Third party evidence is also acceptable under this category.

(para 2) A relevant police caution for a domestic violence offence

Same list of offences as above but he must have received a formal police caution as opposed to an "advice". In reality this may difficult to evidence, particularly if the client was not the victim. Third party evidence is acceptable.

(para 3) Relevant ongoing criminal proceedings

The key here is "ongoing" i.e. not concluded. It must also be in relation to a domestic violence offence against an associated person. It can also relate to proceedings outside of the UK. It can be evidenced by way of newspaper article, letter from the court, police or CPS. Third party evidence is acceptable.

(para 4) A relevant conviction for a domestic violence offence

With same considerations as above and can be evidenced by court, police or CPS. Third party evidence is acceptable.

(para 5) Bind overs connected with a domestic violence offence

As above. Third party evidence is acceptable.

(para 6) Domestic violence protection notice

These are protective orders obtained by the police on behalf of victims. Contained within Sections 24-33 of the Crime and Security Act 2010. DVPNs last for 48 hours at which point it would be expected that a DVPO would have been obtained. Third party evidence is acceptable however in practice the test for obtaining a DVPN/DVPO is that "there must be reasonable grounds for believing that the suspect has been *violent* or has *threatened violence* towards an associated person". The College of Policing state that "threat of violence allows a wide interpretation to include any behaviour by the perpetrator which instils a fear of violence in the victim", so potentially could be used in cases of coercive control where there is no physical violence or criminal damage however not as likely although this deficiency may be remedied to some extent by the new stalking protection orders.

(para 7) A relevant protective injunction

These "protective orders" must be between associated persons and can include non-molestation orders, occupation orders, DVPOs, restraining orders, forced marriage protection orders, and female genital mutilation protection orders. I would anticipate that the Legal Aid Agency will also accept the new stalking protection orders if made against an associated person. Third party evidence is acceptable. Non-molestation orders and occupations orders (which regulate occupation of the family home) do not require there to have been any physical violence and are ideally suited to assist victims of coercive control as they do not require the assistance of the police or CPS either so the victim is not reliant on the police response, which is sadly often lacking in many cases of coercive control.

(para 8) Undertaking

Must be given under s46 or 63E of the Family Law Act 1996. Third party evidence is acceptable however cross-undertakings are not acceptable and it is therefore an important consideration in advising your client whether or not to give a cross undertaking in order to conclude proceedings if this evidence is required for legal aid purposes. I also would question the value of an undertaking in a case of coercive control where lies and manipulation are often a regular feature of the abuse. Why would the perpetrator stand by his "promise" now when he has probably made and broken hundreds of them in the past. In my experience orders are also more likely to be adhered to than undertakings.

(para 9) Finding of fact

Must be a finding in a judgment from a court or tribunal in the UK that there has been domestic abuse. Third party evidence is acceptable. Allegations from an undefended divorce would not be sufficient as no formal finding of fact has been made.

(para 10) Expert report produced as evidence for court/tribunal

Must have been produced as evidence in proceedings in the UK for the benefit of the court confirming that an associated person was assessed as being or at risk of being a risk of domestic violence by the perpetrator. The government definition of domestic violence includes coercive control so this would be included here. Examples would be a Cafcass report, social services report or psychological assessment. Third party evidence is acceptable.

(para 11) Letter or report from an appropriate health professional

The letter should confirm that they have assessed the victim and in their professional judgment the victim has, or has had, injuries or a condition consistent with being a victim of domestic violence. Health professionals can include GPS, nurses, health visitors, dentists, paramedic or social worker. The evidence does not need to name the perpetrator. "A condition" would include stress and anxiety from coercive control.

(para 12) An appropriate health professional referral to a domestic violence support service

The letter must be provided by the appropriate health professional that made the referral, the person to whom the referral was made (i.e. the domestic violence support organisation) or a health professional that has access to the medical records of the client. This can obviously include cases where the client has complained of no physical abuse just coercive control. The perpetrator does not need to be named.

(para 13) Multi-agency risk assessment conference (or other local safeguarding forum)

This requires a letter from any member of the MARAC or other local safeguarding forum which must consist of more than one agency. The evidence must state that the client or a person with whom your client is in a family relationship, such as their child, is or has been at risk of domestic violence from the perpetrator who must be the other party in the case.

(para 14) Letter from an independent domestic violence advisor/advocate

It must confirm that they are providing support to the client as a victim but doesn't need to name the perpetrator.

(para 15) Letter from an independent sexual violence advisor/advocate

As above but bizarrely does state that the perpetrator should be named.

(para 16) Letter from local authority or housing association

The letter must confirm that in their reasonable professional judgement the client or an individual with whom the perpetrator is or was in a family relationship with, is or has been at risk of being a victim of domestic violence by him. The letter must also include a description of:

- the specific matters the officer has relied upon to support their judgement; and
- the support that they have provided to the individual who is, or is at risk of being a victim of domestic violence. Violence would include coercive control.

The victim and perpetrator should be named and domestic violence would include coercive control

(para 17) Letter from organisation providing domestic violence support services

This includes refuges and support services for domestic abuse. The organisation must have been operating for at least 6 months in England or Wales. The letter must be on letterhead, include the name of the victim and a statement confirming that in their reasonable professional judgement, the client was, or is at risk of being a victim of domestic violence and include:

1. a description of both the specific matters the author has relied upon to support their judgement; and

2. the support that they have provided to the individual who either is, or is at risk of being, a victim of domestic violence and;

3. a statement of reasons as to why your client needed the support from organisation or charity.

This would obviously cover cases of coercive control and is often one of the easiest forms of evidence to obtain as the staff are well versed in preparing the letters.

(para 18) Letter from organisation providing domestic violence support services – refusal of admission to a refuge

There is no 6 months operational requirement as above. The letter must be on letterhead and must state the date that the client, or another individual who is or was in a family relationship with the perpetrator who must be the other party to the case, sought refuge but was refused entry. It must state that your client or an individual who is or was in a family relationship with the perpetrator and that she sought admission to a refuge because of allegations of domestic violence by the perpetrator. The refusal may be because the refuge is full or because the victim had other issues which prevented her from accessing refuge.

(para 19) Letter from public authority

The letter must be on letterhead or, where emailed, the evidence must clearly identify the name and details of the public authority. It should confirm that either the client or an individual who was or is in a family relationship with the perpetrator was assessed as being or at risk of being a victim of domestic violence.

The evidence should also include the name of the individual who is, or at risk of being a victim of domestic violence and the name of the perpetrator.

This could be a social services assessment for example or a pre-proceedings letter.

(para 20) Leave to remain in the UK under paragraph 289B of the Immigration Rules

Must be on letter headed paper from the Home Office and specify that your client has been granted leave to remain in the United Kingdom as the victim of domestic violence under Paragraph 289B of the Immigration Rules2, on or prior to the date the application for legal aid was made.

(para 21) Financial abuse

This section is obviously designed to assist victims of coercive control in cases where the above examples of evidence may be difficult for them to obtain as financial abuse is a common tactic in cases of coercive control. Victims may not have accessed help from their GP or a domestic violence organisation and the police are notoriously bad at bringing prosecutions in these types of cases. The type of evidence is not restricted and it is a matter of discretion for the director of legal aid casework. The regulations state "The evidence provided should reflect that the behaviour referred to constitutes domestic abuse i.e. it should be done with the intention to gain power and control over the victim" It also accepts that on some cases the victim may not have access to corroborating documents such as bank statements or letter from food bank and in those cases a narrative statement would suffice.

This list of evidence has been amended on several occasions so it is important to ensure that you are utilising the up to date list and letter template which can be downloaded from the GOV.uk website. Thanks to the Right of Women the list has been expanded over the years and I would urge you to feed back any problems you may have with obtaining evidence to them as there is always the possibility that further changes could be made.

CHAPTER EIGHT
COERCIVE CONTROL AND FAMILY LAW

This chapter is intended to assist the practitioner and victim in dealing with cases involving coercive control within the family court. I have tried to include advice on how to maximise the victim's chances of coercive control being taken seriously by the court and where caution needs to be applied without it becoming too detailed in terms of case preparation, as this guide is intended as an overview and that would be another book in itself.

Whilst the family courts have come a long way over the last 20 years with regard to how they deal with cases involving allegations of domestic violence there is still a long way to go and coercive control and stalking in particular are still dealt with very badly by the Family Court in general.

When I first started practising in family law over 20 years ago domestic abuse was often ignored by the courts unless it was directly involving the child, and finding of fact hearings were rare in all but the most serious cases of physical violence.

Then there was a shift as campaigners highlighted the impact of domestic violence on women and children and there began to be recognition that even overhearing domestic violence was in itself damaging for a child and that domestic violence was a failure of parenting. The Family Court could only see things from the perspective of the child rather than also looking at the safety of the victim and whist I accept that the Family Court should put the interests of the child at the forefront of its decisions, the safety of the mother should also be a vital consideration that is taken into account in every decision, including practical arrangements for contact and Court hearings.

All too often I have heard lawyers, Cafcass officers, social workers and even Judges comment that it is "six of one and half a dozen of the other" or "why didn't she leave if it was that bad?". I would like to say that this was only at the beginning of my career however unfortunately these views are still there, albeit to a lesser extent. Domestic violence training is still much needed in my opinion within the Family Court arena for lawyers, social workers, Cafcass officers, experts, Judges and Magistrates and I am pleased that the issue of the Family Courts and domestic abuse is currently being looked at by the Ministry of Justice through a panel of experts.

The Family Courts should be there to protect adult victims as well as children however in too many cases I have seen victims put at grave risk by their involvement in Family Court proceedings. Comments by professionals within the family court system minimising the impact of domestic abuse, which has the effect of condoning the perpetrator's behaviour, can lead to an escalation in the level and frequency of incidents as the perpetrator feels vindicated and invincible and it can leave victims feeling as though what they are experiencing is normal and there is nowhere for them to go for help. This can lead to them reconciling with the perpetrator or contributing to worsening mental health issues which are in turn held against them. I have seen victims on witness protection schemes have their new names and/or addresses disclosed within reports and court hearings which then requires them to relocate and change their identity once again for which they are then often criticised for "disrupting the children's stability". I have had Clients assaulted on their way to court for a non-molestation order after the Judge had refused to grant a without notice order which meant that the perpetrator then knew the exact date, time and location of where the victim would be for the court hearing. These perpetrators often feel totally incensed that their ex-partners are daring to stand up to them and obtain a protective order and it is a time of hugely increased risk for a victim. Unsurprisingly, in this case the client did not proceed in the court process and completely disengaged from a process she felt had put her in harm's way.

I have seen victims who have taken years to pluck up the courage to finally leave their perpetrator, plan the separation carefully with a domestic violence support worker putting in safeguarding measures wherever possible, only to be dragged back from their new geographic location and to be forced by a Court order to reside near to the perpetrator once again. Perpetrators can also use Family Court orders to find out where their ex-partner has fled to and once the Court has obtained the address of the victim from the benefits agency the address is often inadvertently given to the perpetrator or his solicitor and even if that does not happen the proceedings will automatically be listed at the court local to the address that she has fled to so the perpetrator will know the town she is in.

Too often victims of domestic abuse and rape are cross examined in court about the very personal and devastating evidence of the attack by the very person who carried out the attack. This, understandably, causes huge trauma for victims. Victims are blamed for "failure to protect" with regard to the children when they themselves have been the victims of prolonged and traumatising domestic terrorism. This trauma is rarely acknowledged or understood adequately.

Many victims tell me that the Court process within the Family Courts has been like a form of domestic abuse where they continue to be controlled by the perpetrator, forced to re-live and recount the minutiae of the psychological, physical and sexual abuse they have been forced to endure, blamed for provoking the abuse or not leaving earlier and then punished by losing residence of their children if they fail to prove the allegations to a court which does not seem to understand the dynamics of domestic abuse and why somebody who may have a high flying job can be so down trodden at home and not leave.

For me, what underpins the failures of the Family Court is a failure to understand the essence of, and dynamics of, domestic abuse which is coercive control. This is why men are able to carry out vile acts against their partner and why women don't leave. It is the glue that keeps her there seemingly unable to get away.

The other thing that the Courts fail to recognise on a daily basis is the risk which domestic violence victims are placed at from the perpetrator after separation. Many judges and magistrates seem to believe that once the parents have separated the risk comes to an end, when in reality the risk has increased dramatically. There is often no consideration given to the fact that if a perpetrator has treated his partner in this way throughout their relationship he will not stop just because she has left him. Quite the contrary. He may well stalk her, be abusive to his next partner in front of the children, use the children and the court process to cause maximum distress to his ex-partner, bad mouth her to the children, try to turn the children against her or harm the children as a punishment for daring to leave, use the Court process to obtain information about his ex-partner so that he is able to stalk her more effectively or use the court process to ensure that he is able to see her at court. Very little regard is given to the fear and distress all of this causes the victim as she is too often simply labelled as being hostile to contact.

The police, social services, refuges, domestic abuse services, housing departments and health professionals are using risk assessment tools such as the DASH however the Family Courts not only fail to use them but often pour scorn on them as being nothing more than a self-serving exercise. Yes, they are completed with the victim, using her testimony but victims are the only ones who know what is going on in their lives and how it makes them feel. The assessor can also use professional judgement in completing the assessment and they should only be completed by accredited trainers. Most domestic violence advocates carrying out these risk assessments have many years of experience in dealing with victims so their professionalism should not be derided. An IDVA would not want to refer a victim to a multi-agency risk assessment conference if she felt that the victim was being untruthful.

Cafcass have a number of tools to assess domestic abuse and a specific one in relation to coercive control, however, rarely, in my experience, have clients said they have been utilised by the Cafcass officer and I have never seen one exhibited to a Cafcass report. Risk assessment tools are only effective if the assessor understands the dynamic of domestic abuse and coercive control, has been properly trained on how to use the risk assessment tool and the assessor builds a relationship of trust with the victim.

What is often misunderstood by the Family Courts is that women are actually statistically safer if they remain within a violent or abusive relationship. Most women are killed as they are leaving (or as their partner believes that they are about to leave) or after separation. So when social workers tell clients to leave their violent partner as though it is as easy as going to buy a pint of milk they are potentially putting victims at risk of homicide. Many victims know that subconsciously which is why they are so terrified to leave and often feel safer if they return. They are not wrong.

Statistically, where coercive control and or stalking are a feature of the relationship, it is many times over a more reliable predictor of homicide than physical violence alone.

Two reports by Women's Aid over the last 15 years have shown the dozens of children murdered by their fathers during child contact –

many during Court ordered contact. Yet still the Courts fail to place sufficient emphasis on the need to take domestic abuse seriously.

The case of Re L (contact and domestic violence) [2000] signified the start of a drive within the family courts to recognise the seriousness of domestic abuse, however this was soon drowned out by fathers' rights campaigners in my view, notwithstanding the original practice Direction 12 J which was issued in 2008 which has been more honoured in the breach than the observance.

So how can we help victims to navigate their way safely through the Family Court system? There are a number of things which practitioners can do to try to safeguard victims of coercive control as much as they can and I will briefly discuss some of them below. The best advice would be to ensure that a victim engages a good lawyer who understands coercive control and, if that is not possible, she utilises the knowledge and experience of an Independent domestic violence advocate or Independent Stalking Advocate Caseworker.

Consider a non-molestation order

There is no requirement for there to have been physical violence in order to obtain an order under the Family Law Act 2016. These are useful in that they offer a level of protection to the victim from behaviour which otherwise may be unlikely to be considered to be a criminal offence by the police such as non-physical incidents even though strictly it could be seen as a pattern of behaviour under the criminal coercive control or stalking legislation.

The test set out in the legislation at s42(5) states that the court "shall have regard to all the circumstances including the need to secure the health, safety and well-being of the applicant or any relevant child." This is not a particularly high bar as it is intended that the focus is to be on protection although some judges may need this highlighting to them.

In cases of significant domestic abuse or coercive control I would always consider an application for a non-molestation order on a without notice basis (also known as ex-parte) as I have seen too many clients assaulted or intimidated before an on-notice hearing causing them to back out through fear. You will have to be ready to justify why this is necessary to the Judge however and detail the reasons within the statement.

So how do you justify a without notice application? The test for a without notice order is where it is" just and convenient to do so" (s45) and in making this determination the court will have regard to "all of the circumstances" including:

a) any risk of significant harm to the applicant or a relevant child, attributable to conduct of the respondent, if the order is not made immediately;

b) whether it is likely that the applicant will be deterred or prevented from pursuing the application if an order is not made immediately; and

c) whether there is reason to believe that the respondent is aware of the proceedings but is deliberately evading service and that the applicant or a relevant child will be seriously prejudiced by the delay [involved] in effecting substituted service.

I think that the second test at b) is generally the most relevant in a coercive control case. Remember, women are most at risk of homicide around the time of separation particularly where there has been previous coercive control. The risk factor relates to the loss of control which is likely to be at its highest point when he realises that she has left, has told people about what he has been doing, has seen a solicitor and has issued proceedings to invoke an authority greater than his. This is the time of greatest risk and why on-notice applications can actually put the woman at greater risk than doing nothing as he will feel "provoked" and therefore justified in taking more extreme action.

Non-molestation orders can be tailor-made and expressed in many different ways depending on the nature of the abuse that is being perpetrated but the statement should justify and show why the particular protection is necessary. If the perpetrator has already vacated the family home and the victim has a right to occupy the courts will often also make an exclusion zone within the terms of the non-molestation order rather than requiring a specific application for an occupation order. The orders can prohibit the perpetrator from an area around the home e.g. 200 or 300 meters so that they cannot be sitting stalking them at the end of the street, watching the house and monitoring her movements. Orders can prevent the destruction of property and exclude the perpetrator from approaching schools or her workplaces. Non-molestation orders have also had to move with the times to deal with cyber stalking. As previously said, coercive control and stalking are often very similar behaviours at different points on the time line. Whilst in a relationship it would be seen as coercive control under the criminal law and after separation it would become stalking. Very rarely now do I deal with a case of stalking which does not include an element of on-line stalking. Orders can prohibit any form of contact including via social media and even from googling the name of the victim or attempting to impersonate the victim online. 'intimidate, harass or pester' is a catch-all provision although many courts avoid this provision on the basis that it lacks clarity however I would argue that as "intimidation "and "harassment" are terms used in the criminal law this should not be the case and that these type of provisions are important precisely because they are wide. Often a perpetrator will simply adapt his behaviour to get around the prohibitions of an order. If he is excluded from approaching within 200 metres he will park his car 201 metres away. This is exactly why the term "stalking" and "coercive control" are not defined under the criminal law to endure that all types of behaviours employed by perpetrators to terrorise their victim will be caught and prosecuted. It is unlikely that "being made to eat from a dog bowl" would be included in a definition of coercive control but that is exactly what one of my clients was forced to endure. Coercive control will be tailored specifically to target that particular victim's vulnerabilities and fears to ensure that it is most effective and who would be best placed to know your most intimate vulnerabilities and fears? Your partner. Which is what makes them the most devastating and successful of persecutors.

If a separate occupation order is necessary with regard to the family home too, for example, an order that the perpetrator leaves the home the Court will first of all carryout the balance of harm test which is – if it appears to the Court that the applicant or a child is likely to suffer a significant harm attributable to the conduct of the respondent if an order is not made, the court shall make the order unless the respondent or child is likely to suffer significant harm if the order was made and that harm is as great or greater than the harm attributable to the conduct of the respondent to the applicant or the relevant child if the order is not made.

The court will then go on to consider "all of the circumstances" including the following issues:

1. the housing needs and resources of each of the parties and of any relevant child;

2. the financial resources of each of the parties;

3. the likely effect of any order, or any decision by the court not to exercise its powers to make an occupation order, on the health, safety, or wellbeing of the parties and of any relevant child; and

4. the conduct of the parties in relation to each other and otherwise.

It is important that any statement therefore address the balance of harm test and the above 4 issues.

The case of G v G (occupation order) [2000] is authority for the fact that physical violence is not necessary for an occupation order to be made so they can be utilised in cases of coercive control.

Unlike with a non-molestation order (see below) breach of an occupation order is not a criminal offence and the courts still have to consider attaching a power of arrest – the test for this decision is if the court is "satisfied on the balance of probabilities that the respondent has used or threatened violence against the applicant or relevant child. Indeed, the court 'shall attach a power of arrest to one or more of the provisions of the order unless it is satisfied that the applicant or relevant child will be adequately protected without a power of arrest". In a case of non-physical coercive control you would need to argue that violence should be defined as the government had defined domestic violence i.e. to include coercive control. If this was not successful then it would still be possible to get the perpetrator back to court for a breach of the occupation order on the basis of contempt of court. The maximum sentence for breach of an occupation order is 2 years imprisonment and in my experience the Family Courts were always far more likely to commit someone to prison for breach of a protective order than the criminal courts as contempt of court is taken very seriously.

Breach of a non-molestation order is now an automatic criminal offence and has been since 2007 although a worrying number of police officers still advise victims to "get one with a power of arrest". If broken the police should arrest and the perpetrator should be produced in the criminal court where he faces up to 5 years imprisonment.

The good thing about a non-molestation order is that it is still possible to refer a breach back to the family court to be dealt with as contempt of court if the police do not take action regarding the breach. Obviously it is preferable that the police deal with it as the victim does not have to pay for legal representation and a criminal conviction also produces a criminal record and up to 5 years imprisonment versus the maximum sentence of 2 years under the civil contempt of court jurisdiction.

Having said that the criminal process can be drawn out over many months and many victims say that they feel as though their views are not taken into account. They are not represented within the criminal system whereas within the contempt of court system they have their own solicitor and are more in control of process. In my experience perpetrators are also far more likely to receive a custodial sentence from a judge in the family court than in the criminal courts.

Coercive control-type breaches are again the ones least likely to be prosecuted which leaves many victims at increased risk as the failure to take action often emboldens the perpetrator and leads to an escalation in behaviour once he thinks he can "get away with it". Victims are left thinking that their ex-partner was right when he told her that no one would believe her (a common tactic in coercive control cases) or that the behaviour is normal and she should just accept it. Either way it can lead to many victims stopping ringing the police which again increases their risk. I have seen a letter from a senior prosecutor within the CPS justifying the reason for not prosecuting a clear breach of a non-molestation order on the basis that she had the option of taking it back to the family court for contempt of court and that they could sentence to 2 years as opposed to the maximum of 6 months in the magistrates court. It ignores the fact that the magistrates can and do refer up to the crown court for sentence where appropriate and that the victim deserves to have the crime dealt with under the criminal law and for the defendant to receive a criminal record if convicted as well as the fact that the process of her taking it back to court for contempt was likely to cost her over £10,000.

Use practice direction 12J

One thing you can do as a practitioner assisting a victim of coercive control is to ensure the court follows the guidelines contained in PD12J much of which is obligatory. Don't expect that this will be followed automatically. Its existence is something that most practitioners are aware of but the detail and requirements of it are often forgotten.

I do not propose to go through all of it here as it is readily available online but do not assume that the court will know it or follow it so you need to know it and have it with you at all times!

PD12J is not new and was originally issued in 2008 in response to the Women's Aid report "29 Child Homicides" which documented the cases of 29 children over a 10 year period who had been murdered by their fathers after separating from the mother.

Of these cases some 11 out of the 29 children were the subject of court orders prior to their murder.

It was this report and the response to it in 2006 by Nicholas wall LJ that lead to the original PD12J being issued in 2008. Nicolas Wall LJ's report recommended, inter alia, that the view of Drs Sturgeon and Glaser experts in the case of re L (a child) (contact: domestic violence) [2001] that domestic violence involved "a very serious and significant failure in parenting – failure to protect the child and failure to protect the child emotionally (and in some cases physically) – which meets any definition of child abuse" was observed by the family court rather than following the flawed notion that contact could be safe if the domestic abuse had only been perpetrated against the mother rather than the child. Whilst the notion of coercive control was not common place at this time it would be difficult to see how non-physical domestic abuse, which falls within the government definition of domestic violence in any event, could be differentiated.

PD12 J was issued in 2008, revised in 2014 due to research which demonstrated that the practice direction was not being implemented consistently by the courts and finding of fact hearing, were not taking place as directed even though the practice direction was not discretionary.

One of the 2014 amendments was to expand the definition of domestic abuse to include coercive control even though at this time coercive control was not yet a criminal offence.

Notwithstanding the amendments and the re-issuing of practice direction 12 J in 2014, the practice direction continued to be routinely ignored by many courts and it took yet another tragic report from Women's Aid in 2016 entitled "19 Child Homicides "which studied the deaths of a further 19 children killed by their fathers during child contact arrangements. This time 12 out of 19 of the children had been murdered during court ordered contact which is hardly surprising on the basis that PD12J was being ignored.

It was Mr Justice Cobb who prepared a review of PD12J this time and unfortunately found many of the failings highlighted in earlier reviews were continuing.

The further amended PD12J came into effect on 2 October 2017 and the phrase "domestic violence "was changed to "domestic abuse" to focus the mind that non-physical forms of abuse are equally relevant in determining risk and how a case should be dealt with.

The new definition states that "domestic abuse includes any incident or pattern or incidence of controlling, coercive or threatening behaviour, violence or abuse between those aged 16 or over who are or have been intimate partners or family members regardless of gender or sexuality. This can encompass, but is not limited to, psychological, physical, sexual, financial, or emotional abuse. Domestic abuse also includes culturally specific forms of abuse including, but not limited to, forced marriage, honour based violence, dowry related abuse and trans-national marriage abandonment".

The new PD12J also includes an updated definition of "harm "which states that "harm means ill-treatment or the impairment of health or development including, for example, impairment suffered from seeing or hearing the ill treatment of another, by domestic abuse or otherwise" The term "development" is defined as physical, intellectual, emotional, social or behavioural development. The term "health" is defined as physical or mental health, the term "ill-treatment" is defined as including sexual abuse and forms of ill-treatment which are not physical "

The new Practice Direction is certainly trying to hammer home the fact that non-physical abuse is something which the courts need to take more account of.

The new PD12J also states that at the conclusion of a finding of fact hearing the court should make findings about the "nature and degree of any domestic abuse and its effect on any child, parent or the relevant person" which is very different to simply recording the findings with regard to what happened and forces the court to consider the nature of the impact of the abuse on the child and the mother.

It does, however, still rely on the judiciary having a proper understanding of coercive control and the impact of coercive control on children and mothers and in my view many judges are not equipped to do this without the assistance of an expert report. Expert reports in relation to this are rarely used but in my view they should be routinely used in establishing the impact on the child and the mother and the expert report should also include a comprehensive risk assessment to assist the court.

PD12 J does not require a finding of fact hearing to take place in every case where domestic abuse allegations are made. The practice direction only requires a finding of fact hearing where "it is likely to be relevant in deciding whether to make a child arrangements order and, if so, in what terms". This is where the problem lies with PD12 J as it relies on the judge seeing the allegation as being "relevant". If the judiciary does not fully understand the nature and dynamic of coercive control and the impact on the mother and child then victims will continue to be failed. In my experience this is particularly so with regard to coercive control as the effects of this are often underplayed and misunderstood as opposed to when allegations of physical violence are made.

Paragraph 40 does however state that the court should make clear how the domestic abuse has influenced its decisions, particularly when findings have been made but the order has still resulted in contact between the perpetrator and the children. The court needs to explain why it took the view that contact will not expose the child to the risk of harm and is beneficial for the child. This may be an area where practitioners can consider whether the Judge's reasoning in this regard stands up to scrutiny or whether it opens up the possibility of an appeal.

Special Measures

Special measures can make the difference in some cases from a client withdrawing her application or failing to engage in the court process and obtaining the best evidence from a client so that the judge is able to make the correct determination based on the full facts of the case.

This is particularly relevant for victims of coercive control where their life will have revolved around reading and interpreting subtle signals from the perpetrator such as the way he looks at her which will often be sufficient to instil fear into her and control her behaviour.

If the case is purely about physical violence then a victim may feel safe at the other side of the court room knowing that the perpetrator cannot physically get near to her however in the case of coercive control if the perpetrator is able to even just catch the eye of the victim this will be all he needs to instil terror into her and let her know that there will be consequences for her if she tells the court what has been happening in their relationship.

Special measures are the arrangements that can be made to help vulnerable and intimidated witnesses give their best evidence in court. Special measures have been used within criminal courts for some time however they are also now widely available within family courts too.

Examples of special measures include arranging for the victim to have a separate waiting area from the perpetrator and his family, a separate entrance and exit to the court, a pre-hearing visit to the court so that the victim can familiarise herself with the layout of the court and know what to expect. One of the most important special measures in my view is the provision of screens to enable a victim to give evidence without the perpetrator being able to get eye contact with her and without the victim being able to see the perpetrator whilst still allowing for the judge, jury or magistrates to see the victim. Another alternative option to this is for the victim to give evidence via a live video link from another room; whilst this is obviously preferable to the victim not giving evidence at all I would always advise that if a client is able to she is better to give evidence from behind a screen as I think that it is important that the judge can "feel "the fear and anxiety emanating from the victim when she gives her evidence and this is far less apparent in my view via video link evidence.

Within the criminal courts special measures are governed by the Youth Justice and Criminal Evidence Act 1999 and the Code of Practice for Victims of Crime (The victim's Code) which places is a requirement on prosecutors to give consideration to the issue of special measures. This will potentially be turned into a statutory presumption if the Domestic Abuse Bill is successful.

Within the family courts there is no such statutory provision and special measures are at the discretion of the judge and often down to the availability of the facilities or equipment at that particular court.

Although most judges will allow special measures if requested it is not uncommon for this to be questioned by the judge and objected to by those representing the perpetrator on the basis that it creates a "presumption of victimhood" so be ready to justify it. Practice direction 3AA – Vulnerable Persons: Participation in Proceedings and

Giving Evidence was issued in 2017 and Part 3A of the Family proceedings rules places a duty on the court to consider whether a party's participation in the proceedings and the quality of her evidence is likely to be diminished by reason of vulnerability and, if so whether it is necessary to provide special measures.

When considering the vulnerability of a party the court must have regard to domestic abuse within the meaning given in PD12J.

This has given victims a greater likelihood of obtaining special measures in the family Court although it is by no means available as of right.

In many family courts in particular the facilities are dire and victims still have to endure home-made special measures including waiting in the cellar of the court and "screens" which are not fit for propose and allow the perpetrator to lean around and make eye contact with the victim.

Requests for special measures need to be made early, in writing, and, if possible, recorded in the court order to ensure that they are available on the day.

Cross-examination of victims by perpetrators

This is another area in which the criminal courts are streets ahead of the family courts. In criminal proceedings the court can make an order preventing an unrepresented defendant cross-examining the victim himself. In family proceedings there is no such order but judges can use their general case management powers to prevent a victim from being cross-examined in person by the alleged perpetrator, however, the family court currently cannot appoint a legal representative to represent the victim and conduct the cross-examination in their place and there are still too many examples of victims still being Cross examined by the perpetrator in family Court. In many cases the judge will be forced to ask the questions to the victim on behalf of the victim but this can give the impression to the victim that the judge is taking the side of the perpetrator so is far from ideal.

Theresa May's domestic abuse bill pledged to deal with this issue however it remains to be seen whether it will see the light of day.

Use the Children Act

The Children Act 1989 was updated in 2005 by the 2002 Adoption and Children Act to amend the definition of "harm" in acknowledgement of the impact on children witnessing domestic violence.

The updated definition of harm states that "Harm" means ill-treatment all the impairment of health or development including, for example, impairment suffered from seeing or hearing the ill treatment of another.

Ill-treatment is defined as including "sexual abuse and forms of ill-treatment which are not physical".

This therefore makes it clear that witnessing coercive control would be considered as "harm".

"Significant harm" is of course the main element of the test in making a care order and the notion of "harm" is relevant in considering the welfare checklist at s 1(3) of the Children Act.

This checklist must be addressed by the court in making any decisions regarding a child in relation to any applications under section 8 of the children act - a child arrangements order also known as residence and contact, a prohibited steps order or a specific issue order.

When the court orders a Cafcass report the Cafcass officer must also address the welfare checklist in relation to the child within the report.

The particular section of the welfare checklist that is relevant in cases of coercive control is section 1 (3) (e) - "any harm which he has suffered or is at risk of suffering ".

The definition of "harm "clearly places an onus on Cafcass and the court to address the issue of coercive control. Paragraph 1 (3)(a) is also relevant in that it requires the "ascertainable wishes and feelings of the child to be obtained in light of his age and understanding." This allows for the child's views to be taken into account particularly if they have witnessed the abuse and it would corroborate the mothers allegations. In cases where the abuse has been more concealed however, it could be argued that the child's views are not informed due to their lack of understanding of the abuse that was occurring. Even where child has witnessed their father committing domestic abuse against their mother it is difficult for a child to truly understand this and certainly they would be unlikely to be able to understand the risk associated with it or the long term impact.

Paragraph 1 (3) (b) is also likely to be relevant in that it addresses the child's "emotional needs" which can rarely be met by a perpetrator of abuse.

Paragraph 1(3)(f) is also relevant in that this addresses "how capable each parent is of meeting the child's needs" – again it is hard to argue that a perpetrator of coercive control – which is a failure of parenting – can be said to be meeting a child's needs which are much more than purely practical.

It is important that the seriousness of coercive control is constantly highlighted to Cafcass and the Judge as still all too often this issue is minimised and the assumption that contact at all costs is best often overrides all other considerations.

One of the ways to do this is at the very beginning of a case. In cases of coercive control I would never recommend mediation and indeed, coercive control is an exemption to the requirement to attend mediation before commencing family court proceedings or applying for legal aid. In a case where coercive control has been a feature mediation will simply be used as an arena to continue to terrorise and intimidate the victim into withdrawing her application.

When issuing the application at court it is important that the court is immediately notified that this is a case of coercive control and should therefore be treated differently as practice direction 12 J will apply.

The means of achieving this is by filing the form C1A – Allegations of harm and domestic violence. This form allows for the applicant to tick several boxes to show the type of abuse they have experienced – physical, emotional, psychological, sexual or financial.

The form also invites the applicant to give a brief description of what has happened and what help they have sought in relation to the abuse.

There is also a box to allow for the applicant to give a short statement outlining any concerns she has about the safety and well-being of the child and what protective orders she believes are relevant.

As soon as the application is seen by the Judge and the Cafcass officer appointed to carry out the initial safeguarding checks at the beginning of the case it should be clear that this is a PD12J case.

The applicant will get an opportunity to file a detailed statement setting out the context and dynamic of the relationship and in cases of coercive control this statement is likely to need to be much longer than a case where physical violence was the main feature. The reason for this is because coercive control is about many examples of behaviour which build up over time until every important aspect of the victims' life is controlled. It is the constant 'drip drip' effect of the behaviour which grinds the victim down over time rather than a handful of extreme incidences.

In recognition of this it may be worth highlighting this to the judge and requesting that the restriction on the length of statements to 25 pages by practice direction 27A be varied.

Likewise, when it comes to agreeing the schedule of allegations and the number of allegations contained within it, which are often restricted to a handful of allegations, it is worth highlighting to the court that a coercive control case will need to show more examples of behaviour than a physical domestic abuse case.

NB – Beware the Family Court

The Family Court is not always a victim's friend and practitioners assisting victims of coercive control need to be aware of orders requiring a person or agency to disclose the whereabouts of a child.

Victims of coercive control may take many years to build up the confidence to dare to separate from the perpetrator and when they do they often want to be as far away from him as possible. The problem for the victim is when they have a child together this makes it very easy for the perpetrator to find her.

All that the perpetrator needs to do is to apply to the court for an order disclosing the child's whereabouts within proceedings for a child arrangements order. These orders are often directed at the benefits agency as often the victim will be claiming child benefit or other benefits in respect of the child and will need to provide an address to the benefits agency. Refuges are often also served with orders requiring them to disclose the whereabouts of the child and therefore the woman. The orders can even be worded requiring "any person" to disclose information including solicitors and, in rare circumstances, against the police. The case of Re B (abduction: disclosure) [1995] held that legal professional privilege can be overridden for the specified purpose of locating a child. An order can also require the solicitor not to inform their client of the order forcing disclosure for a specified period of time so that they are not 'tipped-off' and able to relocate.

The relevant law is contained within section 33 of the Family Law Act 1986.

Whilst these orders should not disclose the woman's address to the applicant perpetrator, it is not uncommon for this to happen. Even if the address itself is not disclosed to the perpetrator the proceedings will then be listed for hearing at the court local to the address of the victim so that the perpetrator will know the location in which she is living and will of course be able to follow her back home after the court hearing which also happens far too often.

If at all possible, it is preferable for the woman to instruct a solicitor based in the location where she resided with the perpetrator to send a cease-and-desist letter requesting that he refrains from attempting to contact her and that any communication should be through solicitors. If the solicitor indicates that they have instructions to accept service this would hopefully negate the necessity to obtain a disclosure order however with a perpetrator of coercive control this may still be something they would want to attempt in any event. If this was the case then this conduct should be highlighted to the court as an example of the perpetrator using the court process to continue to control and abuse the victim.

As highlighted earlier the family courts can be a dangerous place for the victim seeking to keep her identity/ location a secret from the perpetrator as there are risks of accidental disclosure from each individual within the system including the judge, the court staff, solicitors, barristers, Cafcass and any other court appointed experts. It only takes a comment or a document confirming the name of the child's new school teacher or social worker, the new surname they are using or a photograph showing the school uniform or a landmark or shop in the background to provide enough information for a stalker to jigsaw-identify the victim and children. For this reason staying out of the family court arena is often the best policy for victims unless they are required to.

MORE BOOKS BY LAW BRIEF PUBLISHING

A selection of our other titles available now:-

'Ellis on Credit Hire – Sixth Edition' by Aidan Ellis & Tim Kevan
'Tackling Disclosure in the Criminal Courts – A Practitioner's Guide' by Narita Bahra QC & Don Ramble
'A Practical Guide to TOLATA Claims' by Greg Williams
'Artificial Intelligence – The Practical Legal Issues' by John Buyers
'A Practical Guide to Prison Injury Claims' by Malcolm Johnson
'A Practical Guide to Hackney Carriage Licensing in London' by Stuart Jessop
'A Practical Guide to Advising Clients at the Police Station' by Colin Stephen McKeown-Beaumont
'A Practical Guide to Antisocial Behaviour Injunctions' by Iain Wightwick
'Practical Mediation: A Guide for Mediators, Advocates, Advisers, Lawyers, and Students in Civil, Commercial, Business, Property, Workplace, and Employment Cases' by Jonathan Dingle with John Sephton
'Planning Obligations Demystified: A Practical Guide to Planning Obligations and Section 106 Agreements' by Bob Mc Geady & Meyric Lewis
'A Practical Guide to Crofting Law' by Brian Inkster
'A Practical Guide to Spousal Maintenance' by Liz Cowell
'A Practical Guide to the Law of Domain Names and Cybersquatting' by Andrew Clemson
'A Practical Guide to the Law of Gender Pay Gap Reporting' by Harini Iyengar
'A Practical Guide to the Rights of Grandparents in Children Proceedings' by Stuart Barlow
'NHS Whistleblowing and the Law' by Joseph England
'Employment Law and the Gig Economy' by Nigel Mackay & Annie Powell
'A Practical Guide to the General Data Protection Regulation (GDPR)' by Keith Markham

'A Practical Guide to Noise Induced Hearing Loss (NIHL) Claims' by Andrew Mckie, Ian Skeate, Gareth McAloon
'An Introduction to Beauty Negligence Claims – A Practical Guide for the Personal Injury Practitioner' by Greg Almond
'Intercompany Agreements for Transfer Pricing Compliance' by Paul Sutton
'Zen and the Art of Mediation' by Martin Plowman
'A Practical Guide to the SRA Principles, Individual and Law Firm Codes of Conduct 2019 – What Every Law Firm Needs to Know' by Paul Bennett
'A Practical Guide to Licensing Law for Commercial Property Lawyers' by Niall McCann & Richard Williams
'A Practical Guide to Adoption for Family Lawyers' by Graham Pegg
'Essential Motor Finance Law for the Busy Practitioner' by Richard Humphreys
'A Practical Guide to Industrial Disease Claims' by Andrew Mckie & Ian Skeate
'A Practical Guide to the Law of Armed Conflict' by Jo Morris & Libby Anderson
'A Practical Guide to Redundancy' by Philip Hyland
'A Practical Guide to Vicarious Liability' by Mariel Irvine
'A Practical Guide to Claims Arising from Delays in Diagnosing Cancer' by Bella Webb
'A Practical Guide to Applications for Landlord's Consent and Variation of Leases' by Mark Shelton
'A Practical Guide to Relief from Sanctions Post-Mitchell and Denton' by Peter Causton
'Butler's Equine Tax Planning: 2nd Edition' by Julie Butler
'A Practical Guide to Equity Release for Advisors' by Paul Sams
'A Practical Guide to Unlawful Eviction and Harassment' by Stephanie Lovegrove
'A Practical Guide to the Law Relating to Food' by Ian Thomas
'A Practical Guide to the Ending of Assured Shorthold Tenancies' by Elizabeth Dwomoh
'A Practical Guide to Financial Services Claims' by Chris Hegarty
'The Law of Houses in Multiple Occupation: A Practical Guide to HMO Proceedings' by Julian Hunt
'A Practical Guide to Unlawful Eviction and Harassment' by Stephanie Lovegrove

'A Practical Guide to Solicitor and Client Costs' by Robin Dunne
'A Practical Guide to Wrongful Conception, Wrongful Birth and Wrongful Life Claims' by Rebecca Greenstreet
'Occupiers, Highways and Defective Premises Claims: A Practical Guide Post-Jackson – 2nd Edition' by Andrew Mckie
'A Practical Guide to Financial Ombudsman Service Claims' by Adam Temple & Robert Scrivenor
'A Practical Guide to the Law of Enfranchisement and Lease Extension' by Paul Sams
'A Practical Guide to Marketing for Lawyers – 2nd Edition' by Catherine Bailey & Jennet Ingram
'A Practical Guide to Advising Schools on Employment Law' by Jonathan Holden
'Certificates of Lawful Use and Development: A Guide to Making and Determining Applications' by Bob Mc Geady & Meyric Lewis
'A Practical Guide to the Law of Dilapidations' by Mark Shelton
'A Guide to Consent in Clinical Negligence Post-Montgomery' by Lauren Sutherland QC
'A Practical Guide to Running Housing Disrepair and Cavity Wall Claims: 2nd Edition' by Andrew Mckie & Ian Skeate
'A Practical Guide to Digital and Social Media Law for Lawyers' by Sherree Westell
'A Practical Guide to Holiday Sickness Claims – 2nd Edition' by Andrew Mckie & Ian Skeate
'A Practical Guide to Elderly Law' by Justin Patten
'Arguments and Tactics for Personal Injury and Clinical Negligence Claims' by Dorian Williams
'A Practical Guide to QOCS and Fundamental Dishonesty' by James Bentley
'A Practical Guide to Drone Law' by Rufus Ballaster, Andrew Firman, Eleanor Clot
'A Practical Guide to Compliance for Personal Injury Firms Working With Claims Management Companies' by Paul Bennett
'A Practical Guide to the Landlord and Tenant Act 1954: Commercial Tenancies' by Richard Hayes & David Sawtell
'A Practical Guide to Psychiatric Claims in Personal Injury' by Liam Ryan
'A Practical Guide to Dog Law for Owners and Others' by Andrea Pitt

'RTA Allegations of Fraud in a Post-Jackson Era: The Handbook – 2nd Edition' by Andrew Mckie
'RTA Personal Injury Claims: A Practical Guide Post-Jackson' by Andrew Mckie
'On Experts: CPR35 for Lawyers and Experts' by David Boyle
'An Introduction to Personal Injury Law' by David Boyle
'A Practical Guide to Claims Arising From Accidents Abroad and Travel Claims' by Andrew Mckie & Ian Skeate
'A Practical Guide to Chronic Pain Claims' by Pankaj Madan
'A Practical Guide to Claims Arising from Fatal Accidents' by James Patience
'A Practical Approach to Clinical Negligence Post-Jackson' by Geoffrey Simpson-Scott
'Employers' Liability Claims: A Practical Guide Post-Jackson' by Andrew Mckie
'A Practical Guide to Subtle Brain Injury Claims' by Pankaj Madan
'A Practical Guide to Costs in Personal Injury Cases' by Matthew Hoe
'The No Nonsense Solicitors' Practice: A Guide To Running Your Firm' by Bettina Brueggemann
'The Queen's Counsel Lawyer's Omnibus: 20 Years of Cartoons from The Times 1993-2013' by Alex Steuart Williams

These books and more are available to order online direct from the publisher at www.lawbriefpublishing.com, where you can also read free sample chapters. For any queries, contact us on 0844 587 2383 or mail@lawbriefpublishing.com.

Our books are also usually in stock at www.amazon.co.uk with free next day delivery for Prime members, and at good legal bookshops such as Wildy & Sons.

We are regularly launching new books in our series of practical day-to-day practitioners' guides. Visit our website and join our free newsletter to be kept informed and to receive special offers, free chapters, etc.

You can also follow us on Twitter at www.twitter.com/lawbriefpub.